WHAT ON EARTH AM I HERE FOR?

D0873061

RICK WARREN

WHAT ON EARTH AM I HERE FOR?

A SIX-SESSION VIDEO-BASED STUDY FOR GROUPS OR INDIVIDUALS

 **ZONDERVAN®**
.com

 saddleback *RESOURCES*

ZONDERVAN.com/
AUTHORTRACKER
follow your favorite authors

ZONDERVAN

What on Earth Am I Here For? Study Guide
Copyright © 2007 by Rick Warren

Previously published in *The Purpose Driven Life Study Guide.*

Requests for information should be addressed to:

Zondervan, *Grand Rapids, Michigan* 49530
or Saddleback Resources, 30021 Comercio, Rancho Santa Margarita, California 92688

ISBN 978-0-310-69618-6

Scripture quotations marked NIV are taken from The Holy Bible, *New International Version®, NIV®.* Copyright © 1973, 1978, 1984, 2011 by Biblica, Inc.™ Used by permission. All rights reserved worldwide.

Scripture quotations marked CEV are taken from the *Contemporary English Version.* Copyright © 1995 by American Bible Society. Used by permission.

Scripture quotations marked ESV are taken from *The Holy Bible, English Standard Version,* copyright © 2001 by Crossway Bibles, a division of Good News Publishers. Used by permission. All rights reserved.

Scripture quotations marked GW are taken from the *God's Word®* Translation. Copyright © 1995 by God's Word to the Nations. Published by Green Key Books. Used by permission.

Scripture quotations marked KJV are taken from the King James Version of the Bible.

Scripture quotations marked MSG are taken from *The Message.* Copyright © 1993, 1994, 1995, 1996, 2000, 2001, 2002. Used by permission of NavPress Publishing Group.

Scripture quotations marked NCV are taken from the *Holy Bible, New Century Version.* Copyright © 1987, 1988, 1991 by Word Publishing, a division of Thomas Nelson, Inc. Used by permission.

Scripture quotations marked NKJV are taken from the New King James Version. Copyright © 1982, by Thomas Nelson, Inc. Used by permission. All rights reserved.

Scripture quotations marked NLT are taken from the *Holy Bible, New Living Translation,* copyright © 1996, 2004. Used by permission of Tyndale House Publishers, Inc., Wheaton, Illinois. All rights reserved.

Scripture quotations marked TEV are taken from *Today's English Version.* Copyright © American Bible Society 1966, 1971, 1976, 1992.

Scripture quotations marked TLB are taken from *The Living Bible.* Copyright © 1971 by Tyndale House Publishers, Inc., Wheaton, Illinois. All rights reserved.

Scripture quotations marked WNT are from the *New Testament in Modern Speech* by Richard F. Weymouth. Copyright © 1978 by Kregel Publications.

The phrase **Purpose Driven®** is a registered trademark of Purpose Drive® Ministries. All rights reserved.

Any Internet addresses (websites, blogs, etc.) and telephone numbers in this book are offered as a resource. They are not intended in any way to be or imply an endorsement by Zondervan, nor does Zondervan vouch for the content of these sites and numbers for the life of this book.

All rights reserved. No part of this publication may be reproduced, stored in a retrieval system, or transmitted in any form or by any means—electronic, mechanical, photocopy, recording, or any other—except for brief quotations in printed reviews, without the prior permission of the publisher.

Cover inspiration: Brian Montes
Cover image: iStockphoto.com

Printed in the United States of America

17 18 19 20 /DCI/ 26 25 24 23 22 21 20 19 18 17 16 15 14

TABLE OF CONTENTS

A NOTE TO SMALL GROUP HOSTS

This video-based study is designed to be used with a small group of friends at home, at work, or at a church. If you're not already in a small group, start one of your own! It's easy.

How to Start a Small Group

You don't have to be a teacher. You don't need any formal training. You don't even need any experience in a small group. Just keep these four things in mind, and you'll succeed as a small group **HOST**:

Have a heart for people.

Open your home to a group of friends who want to study with you.

Serve them a snack.

Turn on the DVD. The six video sessions by Rick Warren provide the teaching for each week of the study.

If you can do those four things, you can host a small group of your own. All of the material and instructions you need are provided in this study guide. There's no experience necessary, so enjoy the journey!

Please don't feel pressured to discuss every question in every session. There is no need to hurry your way through the material. If your group only has time to talk about what they are learning in *The Purpose Driven Life* book and watch the video lesson together, that's fine. What's most important is that your group members have the time to let God work in their lives. So feel free to select the questions that seem right for your group.

For more information and advice on hosting a small group, see the **Helps for Hosts** section on page 64.

UNDERSTANDING YOUR STUDY GUIDE

Here is a brief explanation of the features of this study guide.

Catching Up: You will open each meeting by briefly discussing a question or two that will help focus everyone's attention on the subject of the lesson.

Memory Verse: Each week you will find a key Bible verse for your group to memorize together. If someone in the group has a different translation, ask them to read it aloud so the group can get a bigger picture of the meaning of the passage.

Video Lesson: There is a video lesson for the group to watch together each week. Fill in the blanks in the lesson outlines as you watch the video, and be sure to refer back to these outlines during your discussion time.

Discovery Questions: Each video segment is complemented by several questions for group discussion. Please don't feel pressured to discuss every single question. There is no reason to rush through the answers. Give everyone ample opportunity to share their thoughts. If you don't get through all of the discovery questions, that's okay.

Living on Purpose: We don't want to be just hearers of the Word. We also need to be doers of the Word. This section of the study contains application exercises that will help your group apply the things you are learning. Be sure to leave time each week for this material.

Diving Deeper: This section contains your weekly reading assignment from *The Purpose Driven Life*. It also refers you to additional resources that will help you grow deeper in your understanding of the purpose you are studying.

Prayer Direction: At the end of each session you will find suggestions for your group prayer time. Praying together is one of the greatest privileges of small group life. Please don't take it for granted.

Small Group Resources: There are additional study materials and small group resources in the back of your study guide.

YOU MATTER TO GOD

SESSION 1
YOU MATTER TO GOD

CATCHING UP

- If this is your first time to meet together as a group, or if you have any new members, be sure to introduce yourselves.

- Before you jump into this study, we recommend that you review the **Small Group Guidelines** on page 70 of this study guide.

- What are you hoping to get out of this study of *What on Earth Am I Here For?*

  I hope to find a clearer image of God's purpose for my life. To develop a closer relationship with Father. To better understand the impact that my purpose can have.

MEMORY VERSE

"I am your Creator. You were in my care even before you were born."

Isaiah 44:2a (CEV)

Watch the video lesson now and follow along in your outline.

YOU MATTER TO GOD

The Question of Existence: Why Am I Alive?

> *Why was I born? Was it only to have trouble and sorrow, to end my life in disgrace?*
>
> **Jeremiah 20:18 (TEV)**

You were made by God and for God's purposes, and until you understand that, life will never make sense.

> *The LORD has made everything for his own purpose.*
>
> **Proverbs 16:4a (GW)**

- God created me to ___love me___ .

> *Long before [God] laid down earth's foundations, he had us in mind, had settled on us as the focus of his love . . .*
>
> **Ephesians 1:4 (MSG)**

The Question of Significance: Does My Life Matter?

> *My work all seems so useless! I have spent my strength for nothing and to no purpose at all.*
>
> **Isaiah 49:4 (NLT)**

"I am your Creator. You were in my care even before you were born."

Isaiah 44:2a (CEV)

You are not an accident. There are accidental parents, but there are no accidental births. There are illegitimate parents, but there are no illegitimate children. There are unplanned pregnancies, but there are no unpurposed people. God wanted you in this world. You are not an accident.

You, [God], saw me before I was born and scheduled each day of my life before I began to breathe. Every day was recorded in your book!

Psalm 139:16 (TLB)

His plans endure forever; his purposes last eternally.

Psalm 33:11 (TEV)

Life is preparation for eternity.

- I was made to *last forever*   .

When this tent we live in—our body here on earth—is torn down, God will have a house in heaven for us to live in, a home he himself has made, which will last forever.

2 Corinthians 5:1 (TEV)

The Question of Intention: What Is My Purpose?

Why did you create us? For nothing?

Psalm 89:47b (NCV)

The only way to know your purpose is to ask your Creator.

Knowing God results in every other kind of understanding.

Proverbs 9:10b (TLB)

- **I find my purpose** <u>in God</u>.

For everything, absolutely everything, above and below, visible and invisible . . . everything got started in him and finds its purpose in him.

Colossians 1:16 (MSG)

Life is not about you; it's all about God

It's in Christ that we find out who we are and what we are living for . . . part of the overall purpose he is working out in everything and everyone.

Ephesians 1:11–12 (MSG)

If you live to be seventy years old, you will live 25,550 days. Don't you think it's worth just forty of those days to find out what you're supposed to do with the rest of them?

"It makes no difference who you are or where you're from—if you want God and you are ready to do as he says, the door is open."

Acts 10:35 (MSG)

40 DAYS

The only way to know your purpose is to ask your Creator!!

t all starts with God. is sostained by God, and ends with God.!!

Discovery Questions

- "God created me to love me." When did you first hear about God's love?

I first heard of God's love from my family as a young child. Didn't realize what that really meant till I was 33 yrs. old.

Please don't feel pressured to discuss every discovery question. It's okay to choose the questions that are right for your group. The point is not to race through the session; the point is to take time to let God work in your lives.

- "I was made to last forever." How does that statement strike you? Are you encouraged, puzzled, disappointed, surprised?

When God looks at me he sees Jesus, not my sins.

- "I find my purpose in God." As you embark on this journey of discovery, how ready are you to explore the truth about God's purpose for your life?

  I am ready, but I am also somewhat scared. Sometimes the things God wants for me are very difficult.

- "Life is not about you; it's all about God." What difference could it make if I acted like life is all about God and not about myself?

  So many instences in my life and indeed my everyday where there is room for more work. I could lead others to Jesus through my actions and testimony.

Living on Purpose

- **Reading Partner:** A central component of this study is the daily reading of *The Purpose Driven Life*. Take a moment to pair up with someone in your group to be your reading partner. A little encouragement and friendly accountability can help you stay on your reading schedule. We recommend that men partner with men and women with women. Check in with your reading partner throughout the week or at your group meetings to share what you are learning, and to encourage each other in your progress through the book.

Now turn to the **Daily Reading Plan** on page 84, and decide as a group the date you will start reading **Day 1** of *The Purpose Driven Life*.

We don't want to be just hearers of the Word. We also need to be doers of the Word. This section of the study contains application exercises that will help your group apply the things you are learning. Be sure to leave time each week for this material.

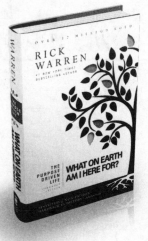

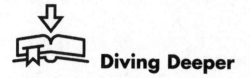

Diving Deeper

- **Spiritual Checkup:** Most people want to live healthy, balanced lives. A regular medical checkup is a good way to measure physical health and spot potential problems. In the same way, a spiritual checkup is vital to your spiritual well-being. The **Purpose Driven Spiritual Health Assessment** was designed to give you a quick snapshot or pulse of your spiritual health. Take three to four minutes alone to complete the **Purpose Driven Spiritual Health Assessment**, found on page 74 of your study guide. After answering the questions, tally your results. Then, pair up with another person (preferably your reading partner), and briefly share one purpose that is going well and one that needs a little work.

- Read chapters 1 to 7 in *The Purpose Driven Life* before your next small group meeting. Share with the world what you are learning by placing a favorite quote from the book on your Facebook page or by tweeting with the hashtag **#PDL**.

- Read the **Memory Verse** on page 2 every day this week as part of your daily devotions. See if you can have it memorized before your next group meeting.

- Visit **www.purposedriven.com** to find suggested next steps in living a life of purpose.

    o Discover **Purpose Driven Leadership Courses** designed to help you learn to fulfill God's purposes in your personal life, small group, and in your church.

    o Sign up for Pastor Rick's free *Daily Hope Devotions* by email.

    o Receive access to 42 audio sermons by Pastor Rick to supplement the message of *The Purpose Driven Life*.

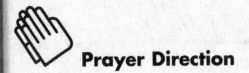

Prayer Direction

• Pray for your group's prayer requests. Be sure to record their requests on the **Small Group Prayer and Praise Report** on page 72.

Before you go . . .

• Turn to the **Small Group Calendar** on page 73 of this study guide. Healthy groups share responsibilities and group ownership. Fill out the calendar together, at least for next week, noting where you will meet each week, who will facilitate your meeting, and who will provide a meal or snack. Note special events, socials, or days off as well. Your Group Host will be very appreciative and everyone will have a lot more fun together.

• Also, start collecting basic contact information like phone numbers and email addresses. The **Small Group Roster** on page 86 of your study guide is a good place to record this information.

WORSHIP

You were planned
for God's pleasure

SESSION 2

[handwritten: ONE Purpose For a Purpose with a]

WORSHIP

You were planned for God's pleasure

CATCHING UP

- Share an insight from your reading in *The Purpose Driven Life* that was especially meaningful to you this week.

  _____

  _____

  _____

- When, where, and how do you feel closest to God?

  I feel closest to God when I am surrounded by other Christians or when I am sharing the word with unbelievers.

MEMORY VERSE

Give yourselves completely to God since you have been given new life.

Romans 6:13b (NLT)

The material in this study guide is meant to be your servant, not your master. If all you have time for is to share what you have read in *The Purpose Driven Life* and watch the video together, that's fine. Don't feel pressured to cover all of the material every week.

Watch the video lesson now and follow along in your outline.

WORSHIP
You were planned for God's pleasure

You [God] created all things, and it is <u>for your pleasure</u> that they exist and were created.

Revelation 4:11 (NLT)

Because of God's great mercy to us . . . Offer yourselves as a living sacrifice to God, dedicated to his service and pleasing to him. This is the true worship that you should offer.

Romans 12:1 (TEV)

- Worship is <u>my response</u> to God's love.
- Worship is <u>giving back</u> to God.

What do you give to a God who has everything? You give him the one thing he doesn't have unless you give it to him. You give him your love.

"Love the Lord your God with all your heart and with all your soul and with all your mind and with all your strength."

Mark 12:30 (NIV)

- **Worship is** _____ **to God.**

That's what it means to "love the Lord your God with all your heart and with all your soul." God wants you to love him passionately.

13

The first reason God put you on earth was for you to get to know him and love him back.

> *He is a God who is passionate about his relationship with you.*
>
> **Exodus 34:14b (NLT)**

> *"I don't want your sacrifices—I want your love; I don't want your offerings—I want you to know me."*
>
> **Hosea 6:6 (TLB)**

The greatest way to express your love to God is by giving your life to him.

> *Give yourselves completely to God since you have been given new life.*
>
> **Romans 6:13b (NLT)**

> *We love Him because He first loved us.*
>
> **1 John 4:19 (NKJV)**

- **Worship is** <u>focusing my attention</u>
  on God.

That's what it means to "love the Lord your God . . . with all your mind." God wants you to love him thoughtfully. God wants your focus because he is focused on you.

> *You have looked deep into my heart, LORD, and you know all about me. You know when I am resting or when I am working . . . You notice everything I do and everywhere I go.*
>
> **Psalm 139:1–3 (CEV)**

> *Set your minds on things above, not on earthly things.*
>
> **Colossians 3:2 (NIV)**

Establish a daily time with God.

> *"Find a quiet, secluded place so you won't be tempted to role-play before God. Just be there as simply and honestly as you can manage. The focus will shift from you to God, and you will begin to sense his grace."*
>
> **Matthew 6:6 (MSG)**

Develop constant conversation with God.

> *Worship him continually.*
>
> **Psalm 105:4b (TEV)**

> *You [Lord] will keep in perfect peace all who trust in you, whose thoughts are fixed on you!*
>
> **Isaiah 26:3 (NLT)**

When you fix your thoughts on God, God will fix your thoughts.

• **Worship is** Using my abilites **for God.**

That's what it means to "love the Lord your God . . . with all your strength." God wants you to love him practically, with your actions.

> *Whatever you do, work at it with all your heart, as though you were working for the Lord and not for people.*
>
> **Colossians 3:23 (TEV)**

It's not what you do that matters; it's who you do it for.

Loving God with my strengths

God doesn't want your compartmentalized life he wants your whole life.

real worship is not an event, it's a lifstyle

> *Take your everyday, ordinary life—your sleeping, eating, going-*
> *to-work, and walking-around life—and place it before God as*
> *an offering.*
>
> **Romans 12:1** (MSG)

Real worship is a lifestyle.

Watch the video entitled, "How to Become a Follower
of Christ." You will find it on the DVD. If anyone in
your group prays for the first time to receive Christ
as their Savior, be sure to take time to celebrate that
decision together.

Discovery Questions

- The Bible says, *Because of God's great mercy to us . . . Offer yourselves as a living sacrifice to God, dedicated to his service and pleasing to him. This is the true worship that you should offer* (Romans 12:1 TEV). What do you think it means to be a "living sacrifice?"

_____

_____

_____

_____

_____

_____

Please don't feel pressured to discuss every discovery question. The point is not to race through the session; the point is to take time to let God work in your lives.

- Surrendering to God is not about losing, it's about gaining. What will you gain by surrendering more of your life to God?

_____

_____

_____

_____

_____

_____

_____

_____

_____

_____

We Need To Be Doers Of The Word

Living on Purpose

- Worship is expressing your affection to God, focusing your attention on God, and using your abilities for God. What is one thing you will do this week to become a better worshiper? Share your plan with your reading partner before you leave this meeting, then connect with each other this week to check up on your progress.

We don't want to be just hearers of the Word. We also need to be doers of the Word. This section of the study contains application exercises that will help your group apply the things you are learning. Be sure to leave time each week for this material.

_____

_____

_____

_____

_____

_____

_____

_____

_____

_____

_____

_____

_____

 **Diving Deeper**

- Do you want to go deeper in worship?

  Visit **www.purposedriven.com/WORSHIP** for **Purpose Driven Leadership Courses**, books, small group studies, and other worship resources for personal and small group use. You will also receive free access to seven audio sermons on worship from Pastor Rick Warren.

- Read chapters 8 to 14 in *The Purpose Driven Life* before your next small group meeting. Share with the world what you are learning by placing a favorite quote from the book on your Facebook page or by tweeting with the hashtag **#PDL**.

- Read the **Memory Verse** on page 12 every day this week as part of your daily devotions. See if you can have it memorized before your next group meeting.

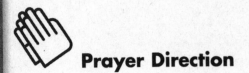

Prayer Direction

- Did anyone commit their life to Jesus Christ after watching Pastor Rick's video message, "How to Become a Follower of Christ"? If so, be sure to celebrate that decision!

- Begin your prayer time by offering short, one-sentence prayers of thanksgiving to God for his blessings in your life. For instance, you might say, "Thank you for my spouse," or "Thank you for my health," or "Thank you for providing for my family," etc.

- Pray for your group's prayer requests. Be sure to record their requests on the **Small Group Prayer and Praise Report** on page 72.

FELLOWSHIP

You were formed
for God's family

SESSION 3
FELLOWSHIP
You were formed for God's family

CATCHING UP

- Share an insight from your reading in *The Purpose Driven Life* that was especially meaningful to you this week.

  _____

  _____

  _____

- Which of these statements is most true of you?

  a) I squeeze my relationships into my schedule.

  b) I plan my relationships into my schedule.

  _B_____

  _____

MEMORY VERSE

You are members of God's very own family . . . and you belong in God's household with every other Christian.

Ephesians 2:19b (TLB)

Watch the video lesson now and follow along in your outline.

FELLOWSHIP
You were formed for God's family

God doesn't just want you to know and love him, he also wants you to know and love his family.

> That family is the church of the living God.
>
> **1 Timothy 3:15b (NCV)**

> [God's] unchanging plan has always been to adopt us into his own family by bringing us to himself through Jesus Christ.
>
> **Ephesians 1:5 (NLT)**

> But all who received [Jesus Christ], to them—that is, to those who trust in His name—He has given the privilege of becoming children of God.
>
> **John 1:12 (WNT)**

> "I am giving you a new commandment: Love each other. Just as I have loved you, you should love each other. Your love for one another will prove to the world that you are my disciples."
>
> **John 13:34–35 (NLT)**

The number one reason God wants us to love each other is so the world will see our love and will want to become a part of God's family too. God wants us to love each other because other people's eternal destinies are at stake.

The Four Levels of Fellowship

- The Fellowship of ___Sharing___ Together

  *All the believers met together constantly and shared everything
  with each other.*

  Acts 2:44 (TLB)

  *Let us not give up the habit of meeting together . . . Instead, let us
  encourage one another . . .*

  Hebrews 10:25 (TEV)

  Open your homes to each other, without complaining.

  1 Peter 4:9 (NCV)

When you let people into your home, you let them into your life. You can't learn
to love people if you're always shutting them out.

  o Share your ___experiences___

  *When you gather . . . each one of you be prepared with something
  that will be useful for all: Sing a hymn, teach a lesson, tell a
  story, lead a prayer, provide an insight . . . Take your turn, no one
  person taking over . . . and you all learn from each other.*

  1 Corinthian 14:26–31 (MSG)

  o Share your ___Support___

  Rejoice with those who rejoice, and weep with those who weep.

  Romans 12:15 (NKJV)

when you share your joy your joy is doubled
when you share your burden, your burden is
cut in half.

Small group life

- The Fellowship of _Beleiving_ Together

God wants every one of us to belong to a church family.

> *You are members of God's very own family . . . and you belong in God's household with every other Christian.*
>
> **Ephesians 2:19b (TLB)**

Being a Christian is more than just believing—it's belonging. Without a church, you don't have a spiritual home.

> *In Christ we who are many form one body, and each member belongs to all the others.*
>
> **Romans 12:5 (NIV)**

> *The person who loves God must also love other believers.*
>
> **1 John 4:21 (GW)**

> *Love your spiritual family.*
>
> **1 Peter 2:17 (MSG)**

- The Fellowship of _Serving_ Together

> *We are partners working together for God.*
>
> **1 Corinthians 3:9a (TEV)**

> *Two people are better than one, because they get more done by working together.*
>
> **Ecclesiastes 4:9 (NCV)**

> *The whole body is fitted together perfectly. As each part does its own special work, it helps the other parts grow, so that the whole body is healthy and growing and full of love.*
>
> **Ephesians 4:16 (NLT)**

• The Fellowship of _Suffering_ Together

Share each other's troubles and problems, and in this way obey the law of Christ.

Galatians 6:2 (NLT)

When you serve together, you do your part, but when you suffer together, you share your heart.

If one member suffers, all suffer together.

1 Corinthians 12:26a (ESV)

Be devoted to each other like a loving family.

Romans 12:10a (GW)

We know what real love is because Christ gave up his life for us. And so we also ought to give up our lives for our Christian brothers and sisters.

1 John 3:16 (NLT)

Discovery Questions

• If true wealth were measured by the depth of
your relationships, how wealthy would you be?

_____

_____

_____

_____

_____

_____

_____

_____

Please don't feel
pressured to
discuss every
discovery question.
The point is not to
race through the
session; the point
is to take time to
let God work in
your lives.

• What could you change in your schedule that would give you more time to
build healthy relationships?

_____

_____

_____

_____

_____

_____

_____

_____

_____

_____

- What does your level of involvement in your local church say about your love for God's family?

_____

_____

_____

_____

_____

_____

_____

_____

_____

- How can you help cultivate the characteristics of fellowship in your church and your small group?

_____

_____

_____

_____

_____

_____

_____

_____

_____

Living on Purpose

- **Service Project:** Let's focus on the fellowship of serving together. Take a few minutes to discuss a service project your group can do together. This could be a project at your church, or an opportunity for your group to help a church family or individual in need. Begin making plans to complete this project in the next three weeks.

We don't want to be just hearers of the Word. We also need to be doers of the Word. This section of the study contains application exercises that will help your group apply the things you are learning. Be sure to leave time each week for this material.

Here are a few ideas to get you started:

- ○ Provide meals for a family in need.

- ○ Visit a church member in the hospital or who is a shut-in.

- ○ Take on a maintenance project at your church such as painting, landscaping, or recarpeting.

- ○ Other: _____

_____

_____

_____

_____

_____

_____

Choose a volunteer to coordinate this project for your group.

Diving Deeper

- Do you want to go deeper in fellowship?

  Visit **www.purposedriven.com/FELLOWSHIP** for **Purpose Driven Leadership Courses**, books, small group studies, and other fellowship related resources for personal and small group use. You will also receive free access to seven audio sermons on fellowship from Pastor Rick Warren.

- Read chapters 15 to 21 in *The Purpose Driven Life* before your next small group meeting. Share with the world what you are learning by placing a favorite quote from the book on your Facebook page or by tweeting with the hashtag **#PDL**.

- Read the **Memory Verse** on page 22 every day this week as part of your daily devotions. See if you can have it memorized before your next group meeting.

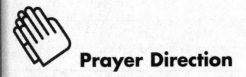

Prayer Direction

- Pray for your small group's **Living on Purpose Service Project**.

- Pray for your group's prayer requests. Be sure to record their requests on the **Small Group Prayer and Praise Report** on page 72.

DISCIPLESHIP

You were created
to become like Christ

SESSION 4
DISCIPLESHIP
You were created to become like Christ

CATCHING UP

- Share an insight from your reading in *The Purpose Driven Life* that was especially meaningful to you this week.

- How are the plans coming for your group's **Living on Purpose Service Project** that you discussed in your last session?

_____

_____

_____

_____

_____

_____

MEMORY VERSE

In all things God works for the good of those who love him, who have been called according to his purpose.

Romans 8:28 (NIV)

Watch the video lesson now and follow along in your outline.

God doesn't just want you to know about Jesus Christ, he wants you to <u>become</u> <u>like Jesus Christ</u>. This has been God's plan for you since the beginning of time.

> From the very beginning God decided that those who came to him—and all along he knew who would—should become like his Son.
>
> **Romans 8:29** (TLB)

> God wants us to grow up . . . like Christ in everything.
>
> **Ephesians 4:15** (MSG)

Three Tools God Uses to Help Us Grow

> In all things God works for the good of those who love him, who have been called according to his purpose.
>
> **Romans 8:28** (NIV)

• God uses *trouble* to teach us to *trust* him.

<u>Trials</u> are situations designed by God to draw us closer to him. <u>They stretch our</u> <u>faith and grow our character.</u>

> Problems and trials . . . are good for us—they help us learn to be patient. And patience develops strength of character in us and helps us trust God more each time we use it until finally our hope and faith are strong and steady.
>
> **Romans 5:3–4** (TLB)

Not a God, but Godly

33

o Every _Problem_ has a _Purpose_ .

The purpose for problems is to make you like Jesus Christ and to build character in your life.

> *"The sorrow in my heart is so great that it almost crushes me."*
>
> **Mark 14:34 (TEV)**

> *"Father" he cried out, "everything is possible for you. Please take this cup of suffering away from me. Yet I want your will, not mine!"*
>
> **Mark 14:36 (NLT)**

Jesus surrendered to God's plan. God wants you to surrender to his plan, too. He is teaching you to trust him in the Gethsemane of trouble.

> Our light and momentary troubles are achieving for us an eternal glory that far outweighs them all.
>
> **2 Corinthians 4:17 (NIV)**

• God uses _temptation_ to teach us to _obey_ him.

Temptations are situations designed by the devil to draw us away from God. God doesn't cause temptation. He never tempts us to do evil. But God can use even our temptations to make us more like Jesus if we cooperate with him. Why? Because every temptation involves a choice. We can choose to do evil, or we can choose to obey God. When we choose to obey God, we take another step in our spiritual growth. Our character is shaped by our choices.

> *Then Jesus was led by the Spirit into the desert to be tempted by the devil.*
>
> **Matthew 4:1 (NIV)**

Even Jesus needed friends!!!...

It is not a sin to be tempted.

> [Jesus] *was tempted in every way that we are. But he did not sin!*
>
> **Hebrews 4:15b** (CEV)

> *The temptations in your life are no different from what others experience.*
>
> **1 Corinthians 10:13a** (NLT)

> *"If you love me, obey my commandments."*
>
> **John 14:15** (NLT)

> *And God is faithful. He will not allow the temptation to be more than you can stand. When you are tempted, he will show you a way out so that you can endure.*
>
> **1 Corinthians 10:13b** (NLT)

Ultimately, it all comes down to your choices. Will you choose to obey the temptation or will you choose to obey God? Every time you choose to obey God, you become more like Christ in your character.

- God uses _*trespasses*_ to teach us to _*forgive*_.

Trespasses are situations designed by other people to hurt us.

> *"Forgive us our trespasses as we forgive those who have trespassed against us."*
>
> **Matthew 6:12**

> *People passing by shook their heads and hurled insults at Jesus . . . and the elders made fun of him . . . Even the bandits who had been crucified with him insulted him in the same way.*
>
> **Matthew 27:39–44** (TEV)

You can't learn to forgive, unless someone hurts you

Jesus said, "Father, forgive these people! They don't know what they're doing."

Luke 23:34 (CEV)

They called him every name in the book and he said nothing back. He suffered in silence, content to let God set things right.

1 Peter 2:23 (MSG)

If you're going to become like Christ, you have to learn to forgive.

o **Remember that God** *has forgiven you* .

. . . forgive others, just as God forgave you because of Christ.

Ephesians 4:32 (CEV)

o **Remember that God** *is in control* .

"You meant to hurt me, but God turned your evil into good to save the lives of many people, which is being done."

Genesis 50:20 (NCV)

God uses trouble to teach us to trust. God uses temptation to teach us to obey. And God uses trespasses to teach us to forgive. He does all these things to make us like Christ.

We go through exactly what Christ goes through. If we go through the hard times with him, then we're certainly going to go through the good times with him!

Romans 8:17b (MSG)

I have been offered drugs once in 3 yrs.

Discovery Questions

- God uses trouble to teach us to trust.
  What problem in your life has brought about
  the greatest growth in your character?

  *Having the power to
  hurt those who hurt
  me and not doing it*

Please don't feel
pressured to discuss
every discovery
question. The point
is not to race
through the session;
the point is to take
time to let God
work in your lives.

- God uses temptation to teach us to obey. What lesson do you think God is
  trying to teach you?

  *To be calm and consider others
  before myself.*

- God uses trespasses to teach us to forgive. What is God teaching you about
  forgiveness right now?

Living on Purpose

- It's never too late to start growing. What progress would you like to see in your spiritual growth one year from now? Pair up with your reading partner and talk about what you can do today to start moving toward that goal.

_____

_____

_____

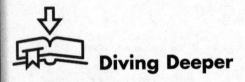

Diving Deeper

- Do you want to go deeper in discipleship?

  Visit **www.purposedriven.com/DISCIPLESHIP** for **Purpose Driven Leadership Courses**, books, small group studies, and other discipleship resources for personal and small group use. You will also receive free access to seven audio sermons on discipleship from Pastor Rick Warren.

- Read chapters 22 to 28 in *The Purpose Driven Life* before your next small group meeting. Share with the world what you are learning by placing a favorite quote from the book on your Facebook page or by tweeting with the hashtag **#PDL**.

- Read the **Memory Verse** on page 32 every day this week as part of your daily devotions. See if you can have it memorized before your next group meeting.

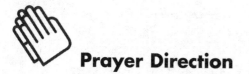

Prayer Direction

- Take turns praying these Bible verses for yourself or for your group.

Example:

God wants us to grow up . . . like Christ in everything.

Ephesians 4:15 (MSG)

Prayer:

"God, please help me to grow up like Christ in every part of my life."
Or "God, please help all of us to grow up like Christ in every part of
our lives."

Now you try it . . .

*In all things God works for the good of those who love him, who
have been called according to his purpose.*

Romans 8:28 (NIV)

*Problems and trials . . . are good for us—they help us learn to
be patient. And patience develops strength of character in us and
helps us trust God more each time we use it until finally our hope
and faith are strong and steady.*

Romans 5:3–4 (TLB)

*Our light and momentary troubles are achieving for us an eternal
glory that far outweighs them all.*

2 Corinthians 4:17 (NIV)

And God is faithful. He will not allow the temptation to be more than you can stand. When you are tempted, he will show you a way out so that you can endure.

1 Corinthians 10:13b (NLT)

"Forgive us our trespasses as we forgive those who have trespassed against us."

Matthew 6:12

Forgive others, just as God forgave you because of Christ.

Ephesians 4:32 (CEV)

- Pray for your group's prayer requests. Be sure to record their requests on the **Small Group Prayer and Praise Report** on page 72.

MINISTRY

You were shaped
for serving God

SESSION 5
MINISTRY
You were shaped to serve God

CATCHING UP

- Share an insight from your reading in *The Purpose Driven Life* that was especially meaningful to you this week.

- Valuable things are not always visible. Name some unseen things that have great value.

_____

_____

_____

_____

_____

_____

MEMORY VERSE

We are God's workmanship, created in Christ Jesus to do good works, which God prepared in advance for us to do.

Ephesians 2:10 (NIV)

Watch the video lesson now and follow along in your outline.

MINISTRY
You were shaped to serve God

There is no such thing as a non-serving Christian.

> *It is he who saved us and chose us for his holy work.*
>
> **2 Timothy 1:9a** (TLB)

God planned in advance what he wanted you to do with your life.

> *We are God's workmanship, created in Christ Jesus to do good works, which God prepared in advance for us to do.*
>
> **Ephesians 2:10** (NIV)

What matters in life is not how long you live but *how* you live. What matters is not the duration of your life but the donation of your life.

God shaped you for service:

S piritual gifts

H eart

A bilities

P ersonality

E xperiences

> *Your hands shaped me and made me.*
>
> **Job 10:8a** (NIV)

Each one should use whatever gift he has received to serve others.

1 Peter 4:10a (NIV)

• My fourth purpose in life is to serve God by ___Serving others___

_____.

Your <u>attitude</u> must be like my own, for I, the Messiah, did not come to be served, but to serve.

Matthew 20:28 (TLB)

How to Serve Like Jesus

• **Serving like Jesus means being** ___available___.

Two blind men shouted, "Lord, have mercy on us."... Jesus <u>stopped</u> and called them. "What do you want me to do for you?" he asked.

Matthew 20:30–32 (NIV)

If you're going to be used by God, you have to be willing to be interrupted.

Never tell your neighbors to wait until tomorrow if you can help them now.

Proverbs 3:28 (TEV)

• **Serving like Jesus means being** ___grateful___.

Jesus looked up and said, "Father, I thank you that you have heard me. I knew that you always hear me, but I said this for the benefit of the people standing here."

John 11:41–42 (NIV)

I thank Christ Jesus our Lord, who gave me strength, because he trusted me and gave me this work of serving him.

1 Timothy 1:12 (NCV)

Serve the LORD with gladness.

Psalm 100:2a (KJV)

• **Serving like Jesus means being** <u>faithful</u> .

don't give up!!!

"I have brought you glory on earth by completing the work you gave me to do."

John 17:4 (NIV)

The one thing required of such servants is that they be faithful.

1 Corinthians 4:2 (TEV)

"For the Son of Man is going to come in his Father's glory with his angels, and then he will reward each person according to what he has done."

Matthew 16:27 (NIV)

Throw yourselves into the work of the Master, confident that nothing you do for him is a waste of time or effort.

1 Corinthians 15:58b (MSG)

"And if you give even a cup of cold water to one of the least of my followers, you will surely be rewarded."

Matthew 10:42 (NLT)

No matter how insignificant your service might seem to you, God sees it all and he rewards it all. In God's eyes, there is no little service.

Whatever you do, work at it with all your heart, as working for the Lord, not for men . . . It is the Lord Christ you are serving.

Colossians 3:23–24 (NIV)

[God] *will not forget how hard you have worked for him and how you have shown your love to him by caring for other believers.*

Hebrews 6:10 (NLT)

• **Serving like Jesus means being** _generous_.

You are familiar with the generosity of our Master, Jesus Christ. Rich as he was, he gave it all away for us—in one stroke he became poor and we became rich.

2 Corinthians 8:9 (MSG)

Out of sheer generosity [God] *put us in right standing with himself. A pure gift. He got us out of the mess we're in and restored us to where he always wanted us to be. And he did it by means of Jesus Christ.*

Romans 3:24 (MSG)

You will be glorifying God through your generous gifts. For your generosity will prove that you are obedient to the Good News of Christ.

2 Corinthians 9:13 (NLT)

You will be made rich in every way so that you can be generous on every occasion, and . . . your generosity will result in thanksgiving to God.

2 Corinthians 9:11 (NIV)

Discovery Questions

- "We serve God by serving others. There is no such thing as a non-serving Christian." What would your church be like if everyone lived by this truth?

There are only two discovery questions in this session so you can spend more time with the Living on Purpose exercise.

- Availability, gratitude, faithfulness, generosity—which of these four attitudes do you need to work on the most?

What did you do with Jesus? What did you do with what God gave you?

Living on Purpose

- **S.H.A.P.E. Profile:** Discover your S.H.A.P.E.! Pair up with your reading partner (see page 8) and complete the "Abilities" and "Personality" sections of the S.H.A.P.E. profile on pages 78 to 82 of this study guide. Then talk about how God might use your abilities and personality traits to serve others. You can finish the rest of the profile on your own this week.

- How are your plans coming for your group's **Living on Purpose Service Project**? Are there any last-minute details that need to be addressed? Make it your goal to complete the project this week.

_____

_____

_____

_____

_____

_____

_____

_____

_____

_____

_____

_____

Diving Deeper

- Do you want to go deeper in ministry?

  Visit **www.purposedriven.com/MINISTRY** for **Purpose Driven Leadership Courses**, books, small group studies, and other ministry resources for personal and small group use. You will also receive free access to seven audio sermons on ministry from Pastor Rick Warren.

- Read chapters 29 to 35 in *The Purpose Driven Life* before your next small group meeting. Share with the world what you are learning by placing a favorite quote from the book on your Facebook page or by tweeting with the hashtag **#PDL**.

- Read the **Memory Verse** on page 42 every day this week as part of your daily devotions. See if you can have it memorized before your next group meeting.

Prayer Direction

- Ask God to lead you into your area of ministry. If you are already actively serving in a ministry, then pray for that ministry right now.

- Pray for your group's prayer requests. Be sure to record their requests on the **Small Group Prayer and Praise Report** on page 72.

Before you go . . .

- There is only one session left in this study of *What on Earth Am I Here For?*
  We hope this study has been a blessing to you. This would be a good time
  to start talking about where you want to go from here in your group life.
  Which of the five purposes do you want to study in more depth together?
  Pick your purpose and then visit **www.purposedriven.com** to find
  more video-based small group studies.

- We also encourage you to plan a seventh session together where you
  can celebrate what God has done in your lives through this small group
  study. This should be a dinner, barbecue, or picnic where the focus is on
  fellowship. It can also be an excellent opportunity to invite other people
  who might be interested in joining your small group. So start making
  plans now.

EVANGELISM

You were made
for a mission

SESSION 6
EVANGELISM
You were made for a mission

CATCHING UP

- Share an insight from your reading in *The Purpose Driven Life* that was especially meaningful to you this week.

- Who is the person most responsible for introducing you to Jesus Christ? How did that happen?

  My mother and grandmother

MEMORY VERSE

Work at bringing others to Christ.
2 Timothy 4:5b (NLT)

Watch the video lesson now and follow along in your outline.

EVANGELISM
You were made for a mission

"In the same way that you gave me a mission in the world, I give them a mission in the world."

John 17:17 (MSG)

What is the difference between your ministry and your mission? Your ministry is in the church. Your mission is in the world. Your ministry is to believers. Your mission is to unbelievers.

"The most important thing is that I complete my mission, the work that the Lord Jesus gave me—to tell people the Good News about God's grace."

Acts 20:24 (NCV)

Two Parts to Your Life Mission

- God expects me to ___*bring*___ people to Jesus.

Aside from your own character, the only thing you will take to heaven with you is the people you have brought to Jesus Christ. Is anybody going to be in heaven because of you?

Work at bringing others to Christ.

2 Timothy 4:5b (NLT)

Build a bridge to the people in your life by finding something in common with them.

Whatever a person is like, I try to find common ground with him so that he will let me tell him about Christ and let Christ save him.

1 Corinthians 9:22b (TLB)

- God expects me to ___go to___ people for Jesus.

"Go everywhere in the world, and tell the Good News to everyone."

God wats us to go!!!   **Mark 16:15** (NCV)

"You will be my witnesses in Jerusalem, and in all Judea and Samaria, and to the ends of the earth."

Acts 1:8b (NIV)

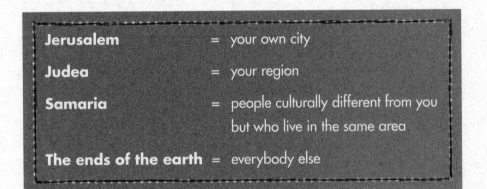

Jerusalem	= your own city
Judea	= your region
Samaria	= people culturally different from you but who live in the same area
The ends of the earth	= everybody else

What Is Our Motivation for Bringing and Going?

- We do it because it's our ___resposibility___.

"Much is required from those to whom much is given, for their responsibility is greater."

Luke 12:48b (TLB)

• We do it because we've been given _Authority_.

> "All authority in heaven and on earth has been given to me. Therefore, go and make disciples of all nations."
>
> **Matthew 28:18–19a (NIV)**

> [God's] intent was that now, through the church, the manifold wisdom of God should be made known.
>
> **Ephesians 3:10 (NIV)**

• We do it because of history's _inevitability_.

> "I have a plan for the whole earth, for my mighty power reaches throughout the world. The LORD Almighty has spoken—who can change his plans?"
>
> **Isaiah 14:26–27a (NLT)**

> "The Good News about the Kingdom will be preached throughout the whole world, so that all nations will hear it; and then, finally, the end will come."
>
> **Matthew 24:14 (NLT)**

The Five Global Giants	**The PEACE Plan**
spiritual emptiness	**P** _planted churches_
self-centered leadership	**E** _equipped servant leaders_
poverty	**A** _Assisted the poor_
disease	**C** _cared for the sick_
illiteracy	**E** _educated the next gen._

The PEACE Plan is a grassroots, church-to-church strategy. It's about all believers in every church doing all of the things Jesus told us to do in the power of the Holy Spirit. It's about churches partnering with churches to take on the global giants in their communities. It's about turning an audience into an army, consumers into contributors, and spectators into participators. Only the church has the manpower, the willpower, and the Holy Spirit's power to do what is otherwise impossible. Jesus has called us, commanded us, and commissioned us to do it. The question is, will you do it? The Great Commission is for every follower of Jesus Christ.

> Send us around the world with the news of your saving power and your eternal plan for all mankind.
>
> **Psalm 67:2 (TLB)**

> [God] does not want anyone to be lost, but he wants all people to change their hearts and lives.
>
> **2 Peter 3:9b (NCV)**

> "Only those who throw away their lives for my sake and for the sake of the Good News will ever know what it means to really live."
>
> **Mark 8:35 (TLB)**

Discovery Questions

- "God expects me to bring people to Jesus."

  Build a bridge to the people in your life by finding something in common with them. Make a list in the space below of five activities you personally enjoy doing. Then write the names of acquaintances who do not know the Lord, whom you could invite to do the activities with you.

Activities	**People to Invite**
(hobbies, sports, work, kids' clubs, dining out, etc.)	*(friends, family, coworkers, neighbors, teammates, etc.)*
Camping	
gardening	
music shows	

Now select one of those activities and make a plan to invite the person/people you listed to do the activity with you. As you get to know them better, look for opportunities to share the love of Jesus with them.

Mark 8:35

• Read the following verses together:

> *Be wise in the way you act toward outsiders; make the most of*
> *every opportunity. Let your conversation be always full of grace,*
> *seasoned with salt, so that you may know how to answer everyone.*
>
> **Colossians 4:5–6 (NIV)**

> *Always be prepared to give an answer to everyone who asks you*
> *to give the reason for the hope that you have. But do this with*
> *gentleness and respect.*
>
> **1 Peter 3:15 (NIV)**

What principles and ideas can you learn from these verses about sharing Christ
with the people you just listed?

_____

_____

_____

_____

_____

_____

_____

_____

_____

_____

_____

_____

_____

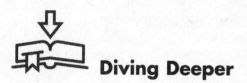

Living on Purpose

- "God expects me to go to people for Jesus."

  You don't have to leave the country to do PEACE. There are PEACE opportunities right here in your own community (Jerusalem), your own region (Judea), and cross-culturally (Samaria). There are poor people all around you who need to be fed, shut-ins who need to be visited, widows who could use some help around the house with repairs or yard work, fatherless kids who need mentors . . . and thousands upon thousands of lost people who need to know the love of Jesus Christ. Take the next few minutes to discuss ideas by which your group can participate in a short-term PEACE project of your own.

Diving Deeper

- Want to go deeper in personal, local, and global PEACE?

  Visit **www.purposedriven.com/PEACE** for **Purpose Driven Leadership Courses**, books, small group studies, and other evangelism resources for personal and small group use. You will also receive free access to seven audio sermons on evangelism from Pastor Rick Warren.

- Read chapters 36 to 42 of *The Purpose Driven Life* during the coming week. Share with the world what you are learning by placing a favorite quote from the book on your Facebook page or by tweeting with the hashtag **#PDL**.

- Read the **Memory Verse** on page 52 every day this week as part of your daily devotions. See if you can have it memorized before your next group meeting.

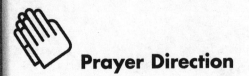

Prayer Direction

- Close your time together by praying for the people you listed above:

  Ask God to strengthen your heart and give you courage to share Christ with them.

  Ask God to give you opportunities to tell them about your relationship with Christ.

  Ask God to soften their hearts and prepare them to hear the Good News of Jesus Christ.

- Pray for your group's prayer requests. Be sure to record their requests on the **Small Group Prayer and Praise Report** on page 72.

Has your life been impacted by this study? Pastor Rick Warren would love to hear how this series and his book, *The Purpose Driven Life*, have helped you. You can email him at: **rick@purposedriven.com**.

Before you go . . .

- Congratulations! You have finished your small group study of *What on Earth Am I Here For?* We hope this study has been a blessing to you. What will you study next? We invite you to visit **www.purposedriven.com** to find suggested next steps in living a life of purpose.

  o Discover **Purpose Driven Leadership Courses** designed to help you learn to fulfill God's purposes in your personal life, small group, and in your church.

  o Receive a signed certificate for having completed *What On Earth Am I Here For?*

  o Sign up for Pastor Rick's free **Daily Hope Devotions** by email.

  o Receive access to 42 audio sermons to supplement the message of *The Purpose Driven Life.*

  o Explore our extensive list of video-based small group studies.

  o Learn how your church and small group can be a part of the PEACE Plan.

- We also encourage you to plan a seventh session together where you can celebrate what God has done in your lives through this small group study. This should be a dinner, barbecue, or picnic where the focus is on fellowship. It can also be an excellent opportunity to invite other people who might be interested in joining your small group. If you haven't already done so, make your plans now.

RESOURCES

Helps for Hosts

Top Ten Ideas for New Hosts

CONGRATULATIONS! As the host of your small group, you have responded to the call to help shepherd Jesus' flock. Few other tasks in the family of God surpass the contribution you will be making. As you prepare to facilitate your group, whether it is one session or the entire series, here are a few thoughts to keep in mind.

Remember you are not alone. God knows everything about you, and he knew you would be asked to facilitate your group. Even though you may not feel ready, this is common for all good hosts. God promises, *"I will never leave you; I will never abandon you"* (Hebrews 13:5 TEV). Whether you are facilitating for one evening, several weeks, or a lifetime, you will be blessed as you serve.

1. **Don't try to do it alone.** Pray right now for God to help you build a healthy team. If you can enlist a co-host to help you shepherd the group, you will find your experience much richer. This is your chance to involve as many people as you can in building a healthy group. All you have to do is ask people to help. You'll be surprised at the response.

2. **Be friendly and be yourself.** God wants to use your unique gifts and temperament. Be sure to greet people at the door with a big smile . . . this can set the mood for the whole gathering. Remember, they are taking as big a step to show up at your house as you are to host a small group! Don't try to do things exactly like another host; do them in a way that fits you. Admit when you don't have an answer and apologize when you make a mistake. Your group will love you for it and you'll sleep better at night.

3. **Prepare for your meeting ahead of time.** Preview the session and write down your responses to each question.

4. **Pray for your group members by name.** Before your group arrives, take a few moments to pray for each member by name. You may want to review the **Small Group Prayer and Praise Report** at least once a week. Ask God to use your time together to touch the heart of each person in your group. Expect God to lead you to whomever he wants you to encourage or challenge in a special way. If you listen, God will surely lead.

5. **When you ask a question, be patient.** Someone will eventually respond. Sometimes people need a moment or two of silence to think about the question. If silence doesn't bother you, it won't bother anyone else. After someone responds, affirm the response with a simple "thanks" or "great answer." Then ask, "How about somebody else?" or "Would someone who hasn't shared like to add anything?" Be sensitive to new people or reluctant members who aren't ready to say, pray, or do anything. If you give them a safe setting, they will blossom over time. If someone in your group is a wallflower who sits silently through every session, consider talking to them privately and encouraging them to participate. Let them know how important they are to you—that they are loved and appreciated, and that the group would value their input. Remember, still water often runs deep.

6. **Provide transitions between questions.** Ask if anyone would like to read the paragraph or Bible passage. Don't call on anyone, but ask for a volunteer, and then be patient until someone begins. Be sure to thank the person who reads aloud.

7. **Break into smaller groups occasionally.** With a greater opportunity to talk in a small circle, people will connect more with the study, apply more quickly what they're learning, and ultimately get more out of their small group experience. A small circle also encourages a quiet person to participate and tends to minimize the effects of a more vocal or dominant member.

8. **Small circles are also helpful during prayer time.** People who are unaccustomed to praying aloud will feel more comfortable trying it with just two or three others. Also, prayer requests won't take as much time, so circles will have more time to actually pray. When you gather back with the whole group, you can have one person from each circle briefly update everyone on the prayer requests from their subgroups. The other great aspect of subgrouping is that it fosters leadership development. As you ask people in the group to facilitate discussion or to lead a prayer circle, it gives them a small leadership step that can build their confidence.

9. **Rotate facilitators occasionally.** You may be perfectly capable of hosting each time, but you will help others grow in their faith and gifts if you give them opportunities to host the group.

10. **One final challenge (for new or first-time hosts).** Before your first opportunity to lead, look up each of the six passages listed on page 66. Read each one as a devotional exercise to help prepare you with a shepherd's heart. Trust us on this one. If you do this, you will be more than ready for your first meeting.

Matthew 9:36–38 (NIV1984)

When Jesus saw the crowds, he had compassion on them, because they were harassed and helpless, like sheep without a shepherd. ³⁷Then he said to his disciples, "The harvest is plentiful but the workers are few. ³⁸Ask the Lord of the harvest, therefore, to send out workers into his harvest field."

John 10:14–15 (NIV1984)

I am the good shepherd; I know my sheep and my sheep know me—¹⁵just as the Father knows me and I know the Father—and I lay down my life for the sheep.

1 Peter 5:2–4 (NIV1984)

Be shepherds of God's flock that is under your care, serving as overseers—not because you must, but because you are willing, as God wants you to be; ³not greedy for money, but eager to serve; not lording it over those entrusted to you, but being examples to the flock. ⁴And when the Chief Shepherd appears, you will receive the crown of glory that will never fade away.

Philippians 2:1–5 (NIV1984)

If you have any encouragement from being united with Christ, if any comfort from his love, if any fellowship with the Spirit, if any tenderness and compassion, ²then make my joy complete by being like-minded, having the same love, being one in spirit and purpose. ³Do nothing out of selfish ambition or vain conceit, but in humility consider others better than yourselves. ⁴Each of you should look not only to your own interests, but also to the interests of others. ⁵Your attitude should be the same as that of Jesus Christ.

Hebrews 10:23–25 (NIV1984)

Let us hold unswervingly to the hope we profess, for he who promised is faithful. ²⁴And let us consider how we may spur one another on toward love and good deeds. ²⁵Let us not give up meeting together, as some are in the habit of doing, but let us encourage one another—and all the more as you see the Day approaching.

1 Thessalonians 2:7–8, 11–12 (NIV1984)

. . . but we were gentle among you, like a mother caring for her little children. ⁸We loved you so much that we were delighted to share with you not only the Gospel of God but our lives as well, because you had become so dear to us. . . . ¹¹For you know that we dealt with each of you as a father deals with his own children, ¹²encouraging, comforting and urging you to live lives worthy of God, who calls you into his kingdom and glory.

Frequently Asked Questions

How long will this group meet?

This study is six sessions long. We encourage your group to add a seventh session for a celebration. In your final session, each group member may decide if he or she desires to continue on for another study. At that time you may also want to do some informal evaluation, discuss your **Small Group Guidelines** (see page 70), and decide which study you want to do next. We recommend you visit our Website at **www.saddlebackresources.com** for more video-based small-group studies.

Who is the host?

The host is the person who coordinates and facilitates your group meetings. In addition to a host, we encourage you to select one or more group members to lead your group discussions. Several other responsibilities can be rotated, including refreshments, prayer requests, worship, or keeping up with those who miss a meeting. Shared ownership in the group helps everybody grow.

Where do we find new group members?

Recruiting new members can be a challenge for groups, especially new groups with just a few people, or existing groups that lose a few people along the way. We encourage you to use the **Circles of Life** diagram on page 69 of this study guide to brainstorm a list of people from your workplace, church, school, neighborhood, family, and so on. Then pray for the people on each member's list. Allow each member to invite several people from their list. Some groups fear that newcomers will interrupt the intimacy that members have built over time. However, groups that welcome newcomers generally gain strength with the infusion of new blood. Remember, the next person you add just might become a friend for eternity. Logistically, groups find different ways to add members. Some groups remain permanently open, while others choose to open periodically, such as at the beginning or end of a study. If your group becomes too large for easy, face-to-face conversations, you can subgroup, forming a second discussion group in another room.

How do we handle the child-care needs in our group?

Child-care needs must be handled very carefully. This is a sensitive issue. We suggest you seek creative solutions as a group. One common solution is to have the adults meet in the living room and share the cost of a baby sitter (or two) who can be with the kids in another part of the house. Another popular option is to have one home for the kids and a second home (close by) for the adults. If desired, the adults could rotate the responsibility of providing a lesson for the kids. This last option is great with school-age kids and can be a huge blessing to families.

Circles of Life

Small Group Connections

Discover Who You Can Connect in Community

Use this chart to help carry out one of the values in the **Group Guidelines**, to "Welcome Newcomers."

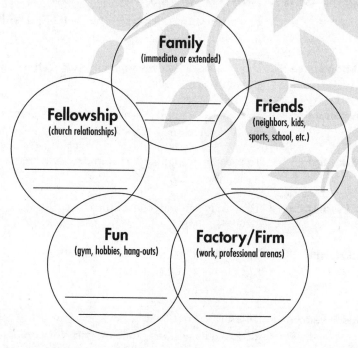

Follow this simple three-step process:

1. List one to two people in each circle.

2. Prayerfully select one person or couple from your list and tell your group about them.

3. Give them a call and invite them to your next meeting. Over fifty percent of those invited to a small group say, "Yes!"

Small Group Guidelines

It's a good idea for every group to put words to their shared values, expectations, and commitments. Such guidelines will help you avoid unspoken agendas and unmet expectations. We recommend you discuss your guidelines during Session 1 in order to lay the foundation for a healthy group experience. Feel free to modify anything that does not work for your group.

We agree to the following values:

Clear Purpose To grow healthy spiritual lives by building a healthy small group community

Group Attendance To give priority to the group meeting (call if I am absent or late)

Safe Environment To create a safe place where people can be heard and feel loved (no quick answers, snap judgments, or simple fixes)

Be Confidential To keep anything that is shared strictly confidential and within the group

Conflict Resolution To avoid gossip and to immediately resolve any concerns by following the principles of Matthew 18:15–17

Spiritual Health To give group members permission to speak into my life and help me live a healthy, balanced spiritual life that is pleasing to God

Limit Our Freedom To limit our freedom by not serving or consuming alcohol during small group meetings or events so as to avoid causing a weaker brother or sister to stumble (1 Corinthians 8:1–13; Romans 14:19–21)

Welcome Newcomers To invite friends who might benefit from this study and warmly welcome newcomers

Building Relationships To get to know the other members of the group and pray for them regularly

Other
_____

_____

_____

_____

We have also discussed and agree on the following items:

Child Care
_____

Starting Time
_____

Ending Time
_____

If you haven't already done so, take a few minutes to fill out the **Small Group Calendar** on page 73.

Small Group Prayer and Praise Report

This is a place where you can write each other's requests for prayer. You can also make a note when God answers a prayer. Pray for each other's requests. If you're new to group prayer, it's okay to pray silently or to pray by using just one sentence:

"God, please help _____ to _____ ."

DATE	PERSON	PRAYER REQUEST	PRAISE REPORT

Small Group Calendar

Healthy groups share responsibilities and group ownership. It might take some time for this to develop. Shared ownership ensures that responsibility for the group doesn't fall to one person. Use the calendar to keep track of social events, mission projects, birthdays, or days off. Complete this calendar at your first or second meeting. Planning ahead will increase attendance and shared ownership.

DATE	LESSON	LOCATION	FACILITATOR	SNACK OR MEAL
	Session 1			
	Session 2			
	Session 3			
	Session 4			
	Session 5			
	Session 6			

Purpose Driven Spiritual Health Assessment

How the Assessment Works

The **Purpose Driven Spiritual Health Assessment** is designed to help you evaluate how well you are balancing the five purposes in your life, and to identify your areas of strength and weakness. The assessment consists of 35 statements that are linked to the five purposes.

Instructions

1. Rate yourself on each of the statements using a scale from 0 to 5, with zero meaning the statement does not match you and five meaning it is a very strong match for you.

2. After you have rated each statement, tally the results by transferring your ratings from each of the statements to the scoring table on this page. Then add up the numbers in each column to find your score for each purpose.

3. Turn to the **Purpose Driven Spiritual Health Plan** on page 77 for further instructions.

My Spiritual Health Assessment

WORSHIP	FELLOWSHIP	DISCIPLESHIP	MINISTRY	EVANGELISM
1. 4	2. 3	3. 3	4. 4	5. 4
6. 3	7. 4	8. 3	9. 4	10. 4
11. 5	12. 5	13. 5	14. 4	15. 3
16. 2	17. 4	18. 4	19. 5	20. 3
21. 5	22. 5	23. 4	24. 4	25. 34
26. 5	27. 3	28. 5	29. 4	30. 5
31. 5	32. 4	33. 4	34. 3	35. 5
29	28	28	28	28

Spiritual Health Assessment

	Doesn't Match		Partial Match		Strong Match	

1. Pleasing God with my life is my highest priority. 0 1 2 3 4 5
2. I am genuinely open and honest about who I am with others. 0 1 2 3 4 5
3. I quickly confess anything in my character that does not look 0 1 2 3 4 5
   like Christ.
4. I often think about how to use my time more wisely to serve God. 0 1 2 3 4 5
5. I feel personal responsibility to share my faith with those who don't 0 1 2 3 4 5
   know Jesus.
6. I am dependent on God for each aspect of my life. .0 1 2 3 4 5
7. I regularly use my time and resources to care for the needs of others. 0 1 2 3 4 5
8. How I spend my time and money shows that I think more about God. 0 1 2 3 4 5
   and others than I do about myself.
9. I am currently serving God with the gifts and passions he has given me.. . . . . . .0 1 2 3 4 5
10. I look for opportunities to build relationships with those who don't 0 1 2 3 4 5
    know Jesus.
11. There is nothing in my life that I have not surrendered to (kept back 0 1 2 3 4 5
    from) God.
12. I have a deep and meaningful connection with others in the church.. . . . . .0 1 2 3 4 5
13. I allow God's Word to guide my thoughts and change my actions. 0 1 2 3 4 5
14. I regularly reflect on how my life can have an impact for the 0 1 2 3 4 5
    Kingdom of God.
15. I regularly pray for those who don't know Christ. 0 1 2 3 4 5
16. I regularly meditate on God's Word and invite him into my 0 1 2 3 4 5
    everyday activities.
17. I have an easy time allowing someone who knows me to speak 0 1 2 3 4 5
    truth to me.
18. I am able to praise God during difficult times and see them as 0 1 2 3 4 5
    opportunities to grow.
19. I often think about ways to use my God-given S.H.A.P.E. to 0 1 2 3 4 5
    please God.
20. I am confident in my ability to share my faith.. . . . . .0 1 2 3 4 5
21. I have a deep desire to be in God's presence and spend time with him. 0 1 2 3 4 5
22. I gather regularly with a group of Christians for fellowship 0 1 2 3 4 5
    and accountability.

	Doesn't Match		Partial Match		Strong Match	
23. I find I am making more choices that cause me to grow when I am tempted to do wrong.	0	1	2	3	4	5
24. I enjoy meeting the needs of others without expecting anything in return	0	1	2	3	4	5
25. My heart is full of passion to share the good news of the gospel with those who have never heard it.	0	1	2	3	4	5
26. I am the same person at church that I am in private.	0	1	2	3	4	5
27. There is nothing in my relationships that is currently unresolved.	0	1	2	3	4	5
28. I have found that prayer has changed how I view and interact with the world.	0	1	2	3	4	5
29. Those closest to me would say my life is a reflection of giving more than receiving.	0	1	2	3	4	5
30. I find that my relationship with Jesus comes up frequently in my conversations with those who don't know him.	0	1	2	3	4	5
31. I have an overwhelming sense of God's awesomeness even when I do not feel his presence.	0	1	2	3	4	5
32. There is nothing in the way I talk or act concerning others that I would not be willing to share with them in person.	0	1	2	3	4	5
33. I am consistent in pursuing habits that are helping me model my life after Jesus.	0	1	2	3	4	5
34. I am open about my weaknesses and see them as opportunities to minister to others.	0	1	2	3	4	5
35. I am open to going anywhere God calls me in whatever capacity to share my faith.	0	1	2	3	4	5

Purpose Driven Spiritual Health Plan

After completing the **Purpose Driven Spiritual Health Assessment**, focus on the areas where you feel you need to plan for growth, and complete this **Purpose Driven Spiritual Health Plan**. Fill in the possible ideas for developing your spiritual life in each area, then translate those possibilities into actual steps you plan to take to grow or develop in each purpose.

PURPOSES	POSSIBILITIES	PLANS (Strategic Steps)
WORSHIP How can I live for God's pleasure? • Regular church attendance • Worship tapes and devotionals • Personal health and balance		
FELLOWSHIP How can I deepen my relationships with others? • Family/friends • Relational/emotional development • Small group community		
DISCIPLESHIP How can I grow to be like Christ? • Spiritual disciplines • Financial stewardship • Character development		
MINISTRY How can I serve God and others? • Ministry to the Body • Leadership training • Continuing training		
EVANGELISM How can I share my faith regularly? • Mission to the world • Seeker friends/family, work, neighborhood involvement		

Purpose Driven S.H.A.P.E. Profile

Spiritual Gifts

The first key factor in discovering your S.H.A.P.E. is to unwrap your spiritual gifts. Review this short list of spiritual gifts from 1 Corinthians 12, Ephesians 4, and Romans 12. As you read through the list, place a check next to any definitions that describe you.* (You may have more than one gift, and everyone has at least one.)

☐ **Administration:** The ability to organize and manage people, resources, and time.

☐ **Apostle:** The ability to sense and seize opportunities to start new churches and oversee their development.

☐ **Discernment:** The ability to distinguish between the spirit of truth and the spirit of error.

☐ **Encouragement:** The ability to strengthen people in their faith and motivate them to action.

☐ **Evangelism:** The ability to preach the gospel in such a way that hearers respond with repentance unto salvation.

☐ **Faith:** The ability to trust and obey God regardless of circumstances, appearances, or risks.

☐ **Giving:** The ability to contribute generously to people in need.

☐ **Healing:** The ability to minister the healing power of Jesus to people who are physically, emotionally, psychologically, or spiritually broken.

☐ **Hospitality:** The ability to make people feel welcomed and to foster biblical fellowship.

☐ **Leadership:** The ability to communicate vision and to motivate others to accomplish a goal.

☐ **Mercy:** The ability to manifest compassionate, practical, cheerful love to suffering people.

☐ **Miracles:** The ability to be used by God to perform powerful acts that glorify God and affirm the truth and power of God's Word.

☐ **Pastoring:** The ability to foster spiritual growth in believers and to equip them for ministry.

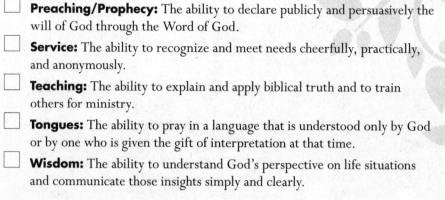

☐ **Preaching/Prophecy:** The ability to declare publicly and persuasively the will of God through the Word of God.

☐ **Service:** The ability to recognize and meet needs cheerfully, practically, and anonymously.

☐ **Teaching:** The ability to explain and apply biblical truth and to train others for ministry.

☐ **Tongues:** The ability to pray in a language that is understood only by God or by one who is given the gift of interpretation at that time.

☐ **Wisdom:** The ability to understand God's perspective on life situations and communicate those insights simply and clearly.

*Some churches define these gifts differently.

Do you have a sense of what your spiritual gifts might be?

_____

_____

Heart

The second key factor in discovering your S.H.A.P.E. is to listen to your heart. Your heart tells you what you are passionate about, and your passions are clues as to where you should be serving. What do you have a passion for?

A role (what you like to do) _____

_____

A people group (whom you like to help) _____

_____

A cause (what you would like to see changed or supported) _____

_____

How can you use your God-given passions and interests to serve others effectively?

_____

_____

Abilities

The third key factor in discovering your S.H.A.P.E. is applying your abilities. Here are just a few God-given abilities. See if you can find any of yours in this list. Feel free to add more in the blanks.

conversing	writing	artistic ability	architecture	engineering
mathematics	baking	coaching	administration	quilting
gardening	athletics	inventing	carpentry	brain-storming
sculpting	selling	public speaking	tailoring	debating
recruiting	organizing	motivating	making music	typing
fixing things	hosting	problem-solving	animal care	listening
teaching	acting	making money	floral arranging	cooking
mechanics	negotiating	decorating	linguistics	videography
other	other	other	other	other

God matches your ministry with your capabilities. How might God use your abilities for ministry?

_____

_____

_____

Personality

The fourth key factor in discovering your S.H.A.P.E. is your personality. Your personality will affect how and where you use your spiritual gifts and abilities. Here are a few God-given personality traits.

1 . . . . 2 . . . . 3 . . . . 4 5
Introvert / Extrovert
(I gain energy from quiet reflection) / (I gain energy from interaction)

1 . . . . 2 . . . . 3 . . . . 4 5
Prefer routine / Prefer variety
(I like to do one project at a time) / (I like to do several projects at once)

1 . . . . 2 . . . . 3 . . . . 4 5
Thinker / Feeler
(I analyze before deciding) / (I go with my gut instinct)

1 . . . . 2 . . . . 3 . . . . 4 5
Work alone   Team player
(I prefer individual assignments)   (I prefer working with a group)

1 . . . . 2 . . . . 3 . . . . 4 5
Structured   Unstructured
(I read instructions before starting a task)   (I start a task and read instructions
                                                      only in an emergency . . . if I can find them)

**How can these personality traits help you discover your area
of ministry?**

_____

_____

_____

Experiences

The fifth key factor in discovering your S.H.A.P.E. is your experiences—both
good and bad.

☐ **Family experiences:** What did you learn growing up as part of
your family?

☐ **Educational experiences:** What were your favorite subjects in school?

☐ **Vocational experiences:** What jobs have you been most effective in and
enjoyed most?

☐ **Spiritual experiences:** What have been your most meaningful times
with God?

☐ **Ministry experiences:** How have you served God in the past?

**What lessons have you learned through your positive life experiences
that can direct you to your area of ministry?**

_____

_____

_____

_____

☐ Painful experiences: God never wastes a hurt. People are always more encouraged when we share how God's grace helped us in our weakness than when we brag about our strengths. What will you do with what you've been through? What lessons have you learned through problems, hurts, and trials? Don't waste your pain; use it to help others.

How might God use the painful experiences in your life to lead you to your ministry?

_____

_____

_____

Now that you have completed your S.H.A.P.E. profile, consider these next two questions:

☐ One of the best places to start serving in ministry is in your small group. How can you use your S.H.A.P.E. to serve your group?

_____

_____

_____

_____

☐ How can you use your S.H.A.P.E. to serve your church? Meet with your church leadership to see what your next step should be in pursuing your area of service to your church.

_____

_____

_____

_____

Answer Key

Session One

- God created me to <u>LOVE ME</u>.
- I was made to <u>LAST FOREVER</u>.
- I find my purpose <u>IN GOD</u>.

Session Two

- Worship is <u>MY RESPONSE</u> to God's love.
- Worship is <u>GIVING BACK</u> to God.
- Worship is <u>EXPRESSING MY AFFECTION</u> to God.
- Worship is <u>FOCUSING MY ATTENTION</u> on God.
- Worship is <u>USING MY ABILITIES</u> for God.

Session Three

- The Fellowship of <u>SHARING</u> Together
  - Share your <u>EXPERIENCES</u>
  - Share your <u>SUPPORT</u>
- The Fellowship of <u>BELONGING</u> Together
- The Fellowship of <u>SERVING</u> Together
- The Fellowship of <u>SUFFERING</u> Together

Session Four

- God uses <u>TROUBLE</u> to teach us to <u>TRUST</u> him.
  - Every <u>PROBLEM</u> has a purpose.

- God uses <u>TEMPTATION</u> to teach us to <u>OBEY</u> him.
- God uses <u>TRESPASSES</u> to teach us to <u>FORGIVE</u>.
  - Remember that God <u>HAS FORGIVEN YOU</u>.
  - Remember that God <u>IS IN CONTROL</u>.

Session Five

- My fourth purpose in life is to serve God by <u>SERVING OTHERS</u>.
- Serving like Jesus means being <u>AVAILABLE</u>.
- Serving like Jesus means being <u>GRATEFUL</u>.
- Serving like Jesus means being <u>FAITHFUL</u>.
- Serving like Jesus means being <u>GENEROUS</u>.

Session Six

- God expects me to <u>BRING</u> people to Jesus.
- God expects me to <u>GO TO</u> people for Jesus.
- We do it because it's our <u>RESPONSIBILITY</u>.
- We do it because we've been given <u>AUTHORITY</u>.
- We do it because of history's <u>INEVITABILITY</u>.

The Five Global Giants

<u>SPIRITUAL EMPTINESS</u>
<u>SELF-CENTERED LEADERSHIP</u>
<u>POVERTY</u>
<u>DISEASE</u>
<u>ILLITERACY</u>

The PEACE Plan

<u>**P**LANT CHURCHES</u>
<u>**E**QUIP SERVANT LEADERS</u>
<u>**A**SSIST THE POOR</u>
<u>**C**ARE FOR THE SICK</u>
<u>**E**DUCATE THE NEXT GENERATION</u>

Daily Reading Plan

WEEK 1: WHAT ON EARTH AM I HERE FOR? (Introduction)   **DATE**

☐ **Day 1**   It All Starts with God   _____

☐ **Day 2**   You Are Not an Accident   _____

☐ **Day 3**   What Drives Your Life?   _____

☐ **Day 4**   Made to Last Forever   _____

☐ **Day 5**   Seeing Life from God's View   _____

☐ **Day 6**   Life Is a Temporary Assignment   _____

☐ **Day 7**   The Reason for Everything   _____

WEEK 2: YOU WERE PLANNED FOR GOD'S PLEASURE (Worship)

☐ **Day 8**   Planned for God's Pleasure   _____

☐ **Day 9**   What Makes God Smile?   _____

☐ **Day 10**   The Heart of Worship   _____

☐ **Day 11**   Becoming Best Friends with God   _____

☐ **Day 12**   Developing Your Friendship with God   _____

☐ **Day 13**   Worship That Pleases God   _____

☐ **Day 14**   When God Seems Distant   _____

WEEK 3: YOU WERE FORMED FOR GOD'S FAMILY (Fellowship)

☐ **Day 15**   Formed for God's Family   _____

☐ **Day 16**   What Matters Most   _____

☐ **Day 17**   A Place to Belong   _____

☐ **Day 18**   Experiencing Life Together   _____

☐ **Day 19**   Cultivating Community   _____

☐ **Day 20**   Restoring Broken Fellowship   _____

☐ **Day 21**   Protecting Your Church   _____

WEEK 4: YOU WERE CREATED TO BECOME LIKE CHRIST (Discipleship)   DATE

- [ ] **Day 22**   Created to Become Like Christ   _____
- [ ] **Day 23**   How We Grow   _____
- [ ] **Day 24**   Transformed by Truth   _____
- [ ] **Day 25**   Transformed by Trouble   _____
- [ ] **Day 26**   Growing through Temptation   _____
- [ ] **Day 27**   Defeating Temptation   _____
- [ ] **Day 28**   It Takes Time   _____

WEEK 5: YOU WERE SHAPED FOR SERVING GOD (Ministry)

- [ ] **Day 29**   Accepting Your Assignment   _____
- [ ] **Day 30**   Shaped for Serving God   _____
- [ ] **Day 31**   Understanding Your Shape   _____
- [ ] **Day 32**   Using What God Gave You   _____
- [ ] **Day 33**   How Real Servants Act   _____
- [ ] **Day 34**   Thinking Like a Servant   _____
- [ ] **Day 35**   God's Power in Your Weakness   _____

WEEK 6: YOU WERE MADE FOR A MISSION (Evangelism)

- [ ] **Day 36**   Made for a Mission   _____
- [ ] **Day 37**   Sharing Your Life Message   _____
- [ ] **Day 38**   Becoming a World-Class Christian   _____
- [ ] **Day 39**   Balancing Your Life   _____
- [ ] **Day 40**   Living with Purpose   _____
- [ ] **Day 41**   The Envy Trap   _____
- [ ] **Day 42**   The People Pleaser Trap   _____

Small Group Roster

NAME	PHONE	EMAIL
1.		
2.		
3.		
4.		
5.		
6.		
7.		
8.		
9.		
10.		
11.		
12.		
13.		
14.		
15.		

The Purpose Driven Life: What on Earth Am I Here For?

Introducing, the 10th anniversary edition of the #1 international bestseller, *The Purpose Driven Life*. This spiritual journey will transform your answer to life's most important question: What on earth am I here for?

Winner of the Gold Medallion Book Award and Christian Book of the Year Award.

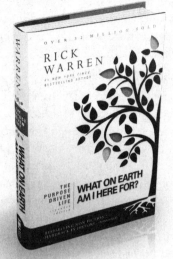

 ZONDERVAN®
.com

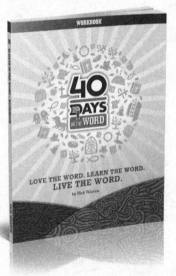

40 Days in the Word

Reignite and strengthen your passion for God's Word! The *40 Days in the Word* DVD and Study Guide are essential resources that take participants through Pastor Rick Warren's six easy to learn methods of Loving, Learning, and Living the Word.

These teachings by Pastor Rick Warren will guide you and your small group through what it means to not just be "hearers" of the Word, but also "doers" of the Word!

saddleback *RESOURCES*
www.saddlebackresources.com

TO ORDER OTHER PRODUCTS BY RICK WARREN PLEASE VISIT
www.saddlebackresources.com

Foundations

Foundations is the Gold Medallion award-winning complete resource for teaching believers the essential doctrines of Christian faith, providing the theological basis for living a purpose-driven life.

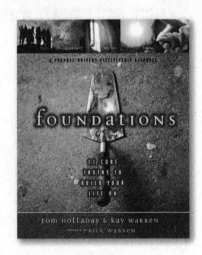

Many Christians today live their lives, plan their schedules, and use their resources completely disconnected from what they say they believe. This spiritual disconnect is the cause of so much of the stress and problems in our lives. Foundations is a fresh, innovative curriculum about the essential truths of the Christian faith and how these truths are to be lived out—in your relationships, your character, and your work. Rather than just teaching doctrinal knowledge, this course shows you how to apply biblical truths and implement them in your everyday life.

Life Management

How do you see your life? How do you make the most of what God has given you? How you see your life will shape your life. Your perspective will influence how you invest your time, spend your money, use your talents, value your relationships, and even face hardships. In this six session study for individuals or small groups, you will learn to see your life from God's point of view, and to worship God by managing your life for his glory.

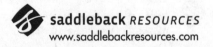

saddleback *RESOURCES*
www.saddlebackresources.com

TO ORDER OTHER PRODUCTS BY RICK WARREN PLEASE VISIT
www.saddlebackresources.com